Look well to the Earth
and the Sea and the Sky—
There's far more to Life
than meets the Eye.

FABLES

Paul David Holman

Northland Publishing

PREFACE

I N FABLES we know that the animals and plants may speak. Here, with a little more license, we find a juxtaposition of forty-three species from Virginia and Arizona, my native and adopted homes. Even in this small community, some are immigrants and each must in one way or another interact with the others.

Fables, from LaFontaine to Joel Chandler Harris, represent collections of ideas from many sources. This collection records observations of human and animal behavior. Some sources are obvious, such as the origin of the stories "I Can Dream" and "A Nonconformist" in Aesop's "The Oak and the Reed" and "The Rival Fishes." Other ideas, such as the smoking tortoise in "The Rings" or the treble clef cattail in "The Singer," may have originated in cartoons seen in childhood or are lost in memory. The first part of the opening couplet may be from an old hymn. Most ideas were simply developed from people's chance remarks, which revealed quirks of character or personality.

Cast the purple shadow of your hand across these pages. Listen as you speak their names. A certain lost familiarity may become apparent as you encounter the crafty Coyote, the bewildered Chipmunk, and the wise Iguana.

PDH

THE WAY OUT

Chipmunk and Groundhog were friends. One day as they were walking along the fence row, Coyote burst out from behind a rock and chased them.

"Quick—follow me!" said Groundhog as he dived into his burrow. Chipmunk made it just in time, tumbling down the tunnel with Coyote nipping at his heels.

Dust filled the air as Goundhog dug deeper and deeper. "How will we ever get out of this one?" squealed Chipmunk.

"Sometimes, my dear Chipmunk, the only way out is deeper in," said Groundhog.

KNOWLEDGE

Owl spent many years involved in the study of the iguana family. He finally thought that he knew all there was to know about them.

"I know more about iguanas than iguanas do," Owl boasted.

"You know more about iguanas than you do about owls," said Iguana.

A NONCONFORMIST

"When I was small," said Red Herring, "my school of fish would be pursued by all manner of predators.

"One fish swam away from the school and was eaten by the pike.

"One fish swam away from the school and was eaten by the bear.

"One fish swam away from the school and was eaten by the eagle.

"But I was actually able to swim away from the school and escape without harm. I have a very pleasant life here in the pond. I wonder if I am considered wise back at the school."

I CAN DREAM

"Your kind has always trailed along the ground, while my kind has always been upright," said the sunflower. "You must always cling to something for support, and I've always supported myself. What have you to say?"

"I can dream," said the morning glory.

That night there was a terrible storm. The ash was blown over and the hickory was uprooted. In the morning, the beautiful sunflower was on the ground with its brittle stem snapped by the wind, and the morning glory opened its blue trumpet to the sunlight.

"What can I do now?" asked the sunflower.

"You can dream," replied the morning glory.

THE COTILLION

A celebration ball was planned after the cleanup
from the great storm. Everyone was to attend. Frog
was very shy and was reluctant to appear.

But on the night of the ball, Frog did appear and
looked very dignified in his evening clothes. When
the crickets began the musical program, Frog was
unable to participate in the dancing because his
arm was in a sling.

"Tell me, Frog," asked the very concerned
Groundhog, "why is your arm in a sling? What's
wrong with it?"

"Shhhh! Come here!" beckoned Frog, who whis-
pered, "Nothing!"

THE BASICS

"What beautiful feathers you have, Bluejay," said Iguana.

"Yes, I preen them in the morning and I preen them in the evening," said Bluejay.

"And what a fine song you sing, Bluejay," said Iguana.

"I trained for years to perfect it. You flatter me," said Bluejay.

"And what a fine nest you have, Bluejay," said Iguana.

"Thank you. I built it myself," said Bluejay.

"May I ask you," said Iguana, "where is your mate, your family?"

"Well, I suppose I have taken care of everything except the basics," replied Bluejay.

THE SOURCE

"What a nice house you live in, Chipmunk," said Owl. "It's so secure and dry and shiny. Where did it come from?"

"From the store," said Chipmunk.

THE CORN FIELD

"Look at that fine field of corn that Turkey has discovered," said Frog.

Turkey pecked his way down a row of corn.

"He's going to get very fat if he eats all of that," said Frog.

Turkey gobbled the corn faster and faster.

"You would think that with all those fine seeds, he could save some to plant next year. He would have the finest corn field ever," said Frog.

Turkey ate all of the corn.

"Frog, it's not the corn. It's the concept!" said Owl.

Feel The Music

"Can't you feel the music, Iguana?" asked Chickadee.

"Well, I can certainly hear the music. I am well aware of the vibrations. I can read the music and sometimes I can even think it. Occasionally, I can even see it. But feel the music as such, no," mused Iguana.

"What do you mean by that?" asked Chickadee.

"It's just a simple fact," said Iguana. "Do all facts have meaning?"

ONE FOR ALL

🐿

"Twenty-eight, twenty-nine, thirty. What are all these big holes in the ground?" asked Turkey.

"As you know, I'm your duly elected mayor," said Raccoon. "Our committees have spent great effort in studying the housing shortage. We have checked the biometrics, the demographics, and the ergonomics. This is what you want, Turkey!"

THE PROVIDER

"Mouse, you are such a good provider," said his wife.

"We always have plenty of corn to eat. We always have the milkweed pods to weave for blankets. We are always safe and dry in our little burrow. We always have such good times here.

"Look at Frog over there. He is always so calm and relaxed. Why can't you be more like Frog?"

THE SINGER

"Listen! What's that awful raspy noise coming from those reeds down by the pond?" asked Chickadee. "Could that be Frog singing?"

"So he thinks," scoffed Bluejay. "Just because one does, doesn't mean one can!"

SO LITTLE TIME

"The world moves so very quickly," said Chipmunk. "And time moves so fast! Some say that nothing matters any more. But there are things that are so important to me. There is so much to learn, so little time.

"Where does the music go when the song is over? What color is the rose at night? What does a gooseberry taste like to a goose?"

"Come here and help me pile up these stones, Chipmunk," said Coyote.

IT'S MINE

"This is my little twig, my perch," said Dragonfly, "and you can't take it. I was here first."

"But it's my twig, too," said Chickadee. "I need it to build a nest. You can find another twig. I need this one."

"Whose twig is it, really?" asked Bluejay.

"It is mine," said the oak tree.

DECISIONS

"Look at Frog on that lily pad," said Bluejay. "What kind of employee is he? He's sleeping on the job again. I asked him if he'd finished that report yet, and all he said was that he's working on it. He shouldn't be paid to sleep on the job!"

"Frog isn't sleeping," observed Iguana. "Frog sleeps much faster than that. It's when he wakes up that he slows down. It's just that decisions are so hard for Frog. If he decides one way, one set of consequences will follow. If he decides another way, another set of consequences will follow.

"Maybe Frog is not really awake, but he never really sleeps, either. Frog is not lazy. He is still gathering data!"

CUMQUAT

"Chickadee, I think it's wonderful that you got that new job you applied for," said Frog. "Does it involve much responsibility?"

"Yes, I'm the new Coordinator for Utilization Management, Quality Assurance, and Time-sharing," beamed Chickadee.

"Allow me to congratulate you," said Frog. "Is that the same as being a secretary?" he asked, not knowing quite what to make of this impressive title.

"I have far more responsibility than that," said Chickadee.

"Then is it the same as being a clerk?" asked Frog.

"Precisely," said Chickadee.

THE JEWEL

The jewel that Chickadee treasured was a very beautiful purple amethyst. She kept it tightly clutched beneath her wings. She stepped carefully along the canyon path, for holding the jewel kept her from flying.

Raven offered her a glistening blue nugget of turquoise, which she refused. The oriole offered her a shining green emerald, which she also refused. Even the little hummingbird tried to give her a bright red ruby, which she refused.

"I don't want to lose you, beautiful jewel," she said.

And the jewel was beautiful. But Chickadee could not see the treasures offered her by the others, as her head was bowed down in clutching the amethyst.

THE TOP LEDGE

"Born a reptile, I was just hatched out by the sun," said Iguana. "Do you know how that feels?"

"What an ignominious beginning," said Owl. "I don't know exactly how that feels, but I can imagine it. At least my family was there when I arrived. Your choices must have been limited from the start."

"Yes, but I chose to perch higher on the hill than my neighbors," said Iguana. "I found that if I went to school I could get up on a ledge where the others weren't allowed. Then I went back to school to get up on a higher ledge. Then I diligently studied for another degree to reach the very top ledge of the cliff."

"I'm very impressed with your accomplishments," said Owl. "What did you find up there?"

"There is very little water," sighed Iguana. "And a dozen other iguanas were already up there. It is never lonely at the top."

CARTWHEELS

"Look, Frog, Chipmunk is making a fool of him-self doing all those cartwheels," said Squirrel. "He's in an absolute frenzy. He will surely get dizzy. He may even get sick from it."

"Why are you doing cartwheels, Chipmunk?" asked Frog.

Chipmunk replied, "Haven't you heard? It's the latest exercise. Everyone down at the pond does it all the time. It is very popular."

"Then how do you do a cartwheel?" asked Squirrel.

"Show me, too," insisted Frog. "I've just got to learn!"

UNLIKE SON

"I found the most interesting little pond for us to visit," said Coyote to his father. "It has deep blue water, tall trees, and tortoises."

"I don't like ponds," said the older coyote. "I don't like deep water. I don't like tall trees. And I especially don't like tortoises. It is so very nice and hot and dry back here in the canyon," he said. "I have spent my entire life getting away from ponds."

PROGRESS

"Hurry up, Chipmunk, we don't have all day on this project," scolded Chickadee. "We must make a lot of progress before Bluejay gets back!"

"Tell me about it," puffed Chipmunk. "Is progress really good?"

"Of course progress is good," said Chickadee. "Why else would we be working so hard?"

"Of course progress is good," agreed Iguana. "For some."

"Of course progress is good," said Owl. "At least, in the short term."

THE PROMISE

One day Coyote decided to speak with Chicken on the path. "If I ever catch you, you will surely be my dinner," he said.

So for many months, Chicken never entered this path.

One day, though, Chicken encountered Coyote while carefully crossing the path. "Please, Mr. Coyote, let me go," said Chicken. "I know you said you would eat me."

"I never told you that," chuckled Coyote. "Not exactly that."

THE CALCULATOR

❦

"I need a new calculator for my algebra class," said Iguana. "It would make it so much easier to keep up with the others."

"You don't need a calculator," declared Raccoon. "Do you suppose that Beethoven needed a music synthesizer? Did Shakespeare use a word processor?"

"I think you missed my point, Raccoon," said Iguana.

"And you mine, Iguana," said Raccoon.

I LOVE YOU

"I love you," said Frog.

"I think I ate too much," said Chickadee.

"Why don't we go down to the pond this afternoon?" said Frog.

"I must go on a diet," said Chickadee.

"So, love, what would you really like to do this afternoon?" asked Frog.

"I don't know," said Chickadee. "What would you really like to do?"

"I don't know," said Frog.

"Then why don't we go down to the pond this afternoon?" said Chickadee.

"I must go on a diet," said Frog.

"I love you," said Chickadee.

"I think I ate too much," said Frog.

GROUNDHOG STEW

"I'm cooking a big pot of soup," said Groundhog. "Would you like some?"

"What kind of soup is it?" asked Chipmunk.

"Why, it's corn chowder, your favorite," said Groundhog. "Would you like some?"

"Does it have corn in it?" asked Chipmunk.

"Of course it has corn in it," said Groundhog. "Would you like some?"

"Does it have potatoes in it?" asked Chipmunk.

"It has potatoes and onions and chile peppers and milk and butter," said Groundhog. "It's very good. Would you like some?"

"Do you have any?" asked Chipmunk.

"Forget it!" said Groundhog.

REALISM

"It's not as if we're even in the same world, Frog. I think you live in fantasy," said Chickadee. "Be realistic. We have very little in common. Do you think we really stand a chance together?"

"I think we belong together," said Frog. "What is real? Of course I live in fantasy. To me, that is real."

NOT INTERESTED

Because Red Herring was always unable to attend the weekly council meetings, Owl was delegated to present to him the latest information.

"Last night we discussed the good of the community," said Owl. "We spoke of conservation efforts and fire prevention."

"I'm not interested in your conservation and fire drills at all," said Red Herring. "I can see why you need the trees, Owl. But if there's a fire, it's cool and wet here in the pond. I surely won't burn up in the water. I'm just not interested, thank you!"

And Owl replied, "Can a fish live in black water?"

THE PAINTER

Tortoise was a magnificent sight with his golden polished shell. He smoked many cigarettes, and each time he bounced up and down as he walked, great rings of smoke issued from beneath his shell.

"Tortoise, you have worked steadily all of your life," said Owl. "You must have painted all the houses in this canyon for the past hundred years. It must be about time for you to retire. What would you like to do now?"

Tortoise pondered the question for a long time. "I would like to paint another house," he said. "The mayor's house."

WORSE OFF

Raccoon was very angry at Bluebird. Every week as he passed her nest he had to remind her to clean up the area. The others considered her little territory an eyesore, and Raccoon's job was to try to keep everyone happy.

"This untidiness has gone on long enough. Today I'll really let her have it," said Raccoon.

"Okay, Bluebird, today is the day," he called out as he came around to her small willow tree.

Bluebird cried, "Please don't be angry at me today. Coyote sneaked up last night and completely tore my nest apart and ran off with my chicks."

THE RINGS

"Raccoon, do you know how well-liked Tortoise is?" asked Owl.

"Of course," said Raccoon. "And what a good worker he is at his age! Why, I spoke with him just yesterday about painting my house."

"Do you know how he always smokes so much?" asked Owl.

"Yes, those smoke rings slowly chugging down the path always announce his arrival," said Raccoon.

"Well, I'm afraid that Tortoise won't be painting your house," said Owl. "Today the rings have stopped."

GET SERIOUS

"Get serious, Chipmunk," said Iguana. "Don't you know there is an overwhelming amount of work to be done around here? How can you be so happy all the time?"

"The end result is the same, isn't it?" asked Chipmunk.

"I honestly don't know about that," said Iguana.

SIMPLE GIFTS

On the occasion of Rooster's birthday, all the birds gathered to celebrate. Bluejay gave him a crown of bright feathers for his head. Raven gave him a bright golden band for his leg. And Chicken gave Rooster her very first egg, perfect in its shape and size.

Rooster put the crown on his head and remarked that such finery would increase his stature among the birds. He put the golden band on his leg and declared that this would increase his wealth. But he looked at the egg disdainfully and strutted directly past such a simple gift.

"Just because the gift is simple does not mean that it was easy," said Chickadee as she considered the magnitude of such a fine egg.

"Just because it was easy does not mean it is simple," said Owl.

THE PRODUCT

To get down to the pond, Chicken had to walk carefully beside a long fence. Behind this fence was an unusually large steer with a brass ring in his nose. He had a most formidable appearance and always rejected Chicken's greetings, even though she tried very hard to be both polite and pleasant.

"Chicken, you're a product," declared the steer. "Society has created you. You have to weigh a certain amount. You have to grow at a certain rate. You must produce a certain number of eggs. There's not an original bone in your domesticated body. How does it feel to be a product?"

"I feel all right, I suppose," said Chicken. "And you?"

DOESN'T BOTHER ME

"Frog, would you like to join Iguana for supper?" asked Mouse. "He has a fine plate of flies he may share with you if you ask."

"No, let's walk along," said Frog. "It doesn't bother me to see him enjoying something that doesn't belong to me."

Presently they encountered Chipmunk, walking with Chickadee along the same path.

"Shall we ask them to join us on our walk?" asked Mouse. "It doesn't bother you to be around that which you can't have."

"Sometimes it bothers me a great deal," said Frog.

WORD FOR THE DAY

"Iguana, surely you're the best-educated one on our council," said Raccoon. "You've studied our emergency plans. You've indicated our evacuation routes and our storehouse capacities. You know everything about our shelters and our weapons. What would you say is the most important thing our citizens need to know in an emergency?"

Iguana slowly nodded his head, acknowledging the question and looking very wise, and said, *"Agua."*

NOW WHERE?

"You would think Chipmunk would be exhausted," observed Coyote. "First, he runs up to that big rock and back. Next, he dashes down to that cactus and back. Then he skitters over to the wood-pile and back. Now where do you think he is going?"

"It is quite simple to figure out where Chipmunk is going," said Owl. "Just look where he has been."

THE BLUE RIBBON

For as long as anyone could remember, the trunk of an ancient cottonwood tree had lain by the side of the pond. One day, Mouse discovered a blue ribbon on one of its branches, although it was crumpled and faded from weather.

"Look, Chickadee," he said. "This must have been here a long time. Perhaps it was a prize for some contest. Maybe it was used to wrap a present. What story do you think it could tell?"

"A lover gave it to someone to tie in a bow upon her head," Chickadee replied sadly. "I know."

THE VACATION

"I'll travel to the pond in the next canyon this year," said Groundhog. "All who have seen it declare that it's quite beautiful. My cousins, the mice, are fortunate to live so close to it."

And so for weeks, Groundhog packed and made plans and studied his map.

Finally, the great day came. Just as Groundhog was leaving, the entire mouse family arrived at his doorstep. "We're here to visit the beautiful waterfall in your canyon," said the mice. "Could you tell us about it?"

"I've never seen it," said Groundhog. "Why don't you visit my waterfall and I'll visit your pond, then we'll meet right here next week."

A week later, the very weary mouse family met the bedraggled Groundhog and told him how exhausted they were. "It's hard work having fun," agreed Groundhog.

WHO'S NEXT

"Who's next?" Bluejay would ask. He had become the most successful attorney in the community and his life was filled with *res ipsa loquiturs* and *ex post factos*. He worked at helping those in trouble and at sorting out good from evil. His office was always crowded with clients. And so he asked of Chickadee, "Do you know who's next?"

"Yes," answered Chickadee. "It is you."